The Papago (Tohono O'odham) & Pima Indians of Arizona

Ruth Underhill, Ph.D.

The Papago (Tohono O'odham) and Pima Indians of Arizona

By
RUTH UNDERHILL, Ph.D.

Illustrated with photographs from
THE BUREAU OF AMERICAN ETHNOLOGY
and drawings by
VELINO HERRERA
(Ma-pe-wi)

Originally published in 1941 by the U.S. Bureau of Indian Affairs as
The Papago Indians of Arizona and their Relatives The Pima

FILTER PRESS, LLC
P. O. Box 95
Palmer Lake, Colorado 80133
2000

Papago (Tohono O'odham) and Pima Indians of Arizona by Ruth M. Underhill, Ph.D., was originally published in 1941 by the U.S. Bureau of Indian Affairs as *The Papago Indians of Arizona and their Relatives the Pima*. This reprint is slightly altered in design from the original publication. Text and illustrations are reproduced here as they appeared in the original.

ISBN: 0-86541-059-3

Filter Press, LLC
P.O. Box 95, Palmer Lake, CO 80133
(719) 481-2420

Contents

Papago home scene: basket making, grinding corn with metate, typical water jar.

THE PAPAGO AND PIMA INDIANS

WHO AND WHERE

WHO ARE THE PAPAGO?

THE PAPAGO live in the hot, desert country of Arizona, on the border of Mexico. It is a land where the sky is bright blue for ten months of the year, with hardly a drop of rain. The thermometer (if you can find one) goes up to a hundred and twenty degrees in the summer. In winter the bright, cool days are about like spring in New England. You could drive over this country for miles without seeing a tree. You would see only gravel, sparkling in the sun, with low bushes spaced far apart, as if in a garden. Plants cannot grow close together here for they would not have water enough to live. On the hillsides, you might see tall cactus, like a forest of bare poles. This giant Cactus, which grows in Arizona, has no leaves. It is nothing but a green stem, ten or fifteen feet high, covered with rows of thorns. After a while, you might see a few little crooked trees, growing by a place where the water flows in the summer rains. In the distance, you would see mountains, looking like piles of rock with nothing green on them.

It does not look like good country for farming. Yet the Papago have been farming here for hundreds of years. They knew how to find the low places where water sank into the ground after the summer rains. They knew a kind of bean which would grow in dry weather—weather so hot that even corn would die. In fact, they knew how to live where no White man could have lived at all, in former days. There were many tribes of Indians who could not have lived there either.

Many Americans, Indians and Whites too, know little about these Indians of southern Arizona. That is because their country belonged to Mexico until about eighty years ago. The Papago bought their knives and their horses from Mexico and, when they learned a White man's language, they learned Spanish. But about 1853 the United States bought some land from Mexico. With the land came some five thousand new citizens—the Papago Indians. They did not look like the Indians the White people were used to. They did not wear feather headdresses nor deerskin clothes nor moccasins. They did not hunt the buffalo. They did not spend their time in traveling, carrying all their possessions with them. Instead, they lived peacefully in villages, raising corn, beans, and squash. They wore clothes which were often made of cotton and they spun and wove the cotton cloth themselves. On their feet, they wore sandals which are flat soles tied to the feet with string. Indians from the north found this so strange that they called them Sandal People.

That was not what they called themselves, however. Their own name was Aw-aw-tam, the People. That was the way with many Indian tribes who felt that outsiders, with different language and customs, were simply not people at all. The People were once a large nation, stretching over the border into what is now Old Mexico. Many of their groups are gone now, some driven out by Apaches, some intermarried with Mexicans. Two groups remain on reservations in the United States. One is the Papago group which we have been telling about, and that lives in the desert. These Indians call themselves Tohono Aw-aw-tam, Desert People. The other group is very close to the Papago in language and customs. We call them Pima (pee-mah).

WHO ARE THE PIMA?

The Pima live north of the Papago, along the Gila River. (Gila is a Spanish word, pronounced Heela!) You might not know it was a river if you crossed it now, for its water has been drawn off into irrigation ditches. But, in old days, it was the one living stream in hundreds of miles of thirsty desert. No wonder those of "The People" who lived along it had a special name, River People. We call them Pima (pee-mah). The real difference between Pima and Papago is that, in former days, the Pima had plenty of water and the Papago had almost none. Except for that, they were almost the same. Our description, most of the time, will hold for both.

We shall speak of them by their modern names, Pima and Papago. If you wonder where these names came from, the answer is, they were given in fun. It happened more than two hundred years ago in Spanish times. We have mentioned that Papago and Pima country was once part of Mexico. It was an almost unknown, northern part and it was years before the Spanish explorers reached it. They thought they were almost at the ends of the earth and they asked the strange Indians many questions. The Indians thought it wise not to talk too much and they answered every question with *pi nyi maach*, I don't know. The Spaniards thought that was the name of the tribe and they wrote on their maps Pima. They used the name in those days for both Pima and Papago. As the Spaniards traveled, they found that the People made fun of some of their number who lived in the desert and called them Bean People. This was because their climate was so hot and dry that, sometimes, they could grow nothing but beans. The Indian words for Bean People are Papavi Aw-aw-tam but the Spaniards found this hard to pronounce and they made it Papago. So we got the names which are on government maps today.

The Spaniards were not surprised to find Indians who wore cotton clothes and spent their time in farming, for that was the usual thing in Mexico. If we could have traveled up that country in former days, from Mexico City to where the United States border now begins, we could choose a route which led most of the way through farming country. The farmers would all speak similar languages, too.

Those who have read the other books in this series have heard the expression language family, and they know that it refers to a group of languages which extends through a western part of the United States, from Montana to Mexico City. The Mexican Indians we have been describing spoke Uto-Aztecan and though they could not always understand one another, their languages at bottom were similar. In a language family, we can have close relatives and distant relatives. The Uto-Aztecan languages of Mexico seem quite close relatives, according to latest studies, and the language of the People is one of them.

North of the Pima, come more distant relatives. We have already heard of the Paiute who are also Uto-Aztecans. So are some of the "Mission" Indians of California. So are the Hopi, the Shoshoni, the Comanche, the Ute. Even some of the Pueblos of the Rio Grande, according to latest guesses, may be very distant relatives. But the Gila River is a real boundary line separating the farmers and irrigators, with the Mexican games and ceremonies, from the wilder people to the north, who usually wandered about gathering their food.

We began by speaking of the People as farmers and this fact is one of the most important in our story. Ruins tell us that there was corn in the country of the Papago and Pima twelve hundred years ago and probably more. There was irrigation a thousand years ago. Was it these very Papago and Pima who did such important work: Were they the first farmers in the Southwest? Some students think so and all of them eagerly watch the digging to get the answer. We shall not attempt to guess it here for more facts are needed before we can be sure. All we shall give is a picture of Papago life as it must have been just before the coming of the White man. In many parts of Papago country it is still very much like that, though changes are coming fast. In the final pages we shall tell what has happened in the hundred and fifty years since the first Spaniards came.

HOW AND WHAT

HOW DID THEY LIVE?

IN THE country of the Desert People, there are no running streams. For three months in the summer, there are heavy rains almost every day and then the dry valleys blossom with plants. During this time the Papago used to live in the valleys, in regular villages and each family had a house to which it returned every year. Each village was placed near the mouth of a "wash." (A "wash" in the Southwest is a dry stream bed where the water runs after a rain.) The Papago had their fields just below the mouth of the stream bed where the water would soak them every time the wash "ran." Their houses were on higher ground where they would not be wet. They dug a large, shallow hole somewhere near the village. This was to catch the rainwater so they could have it for drinking and washing. The summer villages still have ponds like this and most people called them by a Spanish name *charco*.

About the end of August, the rain stopped. Then the charco began to dry up, little by little. It took quite a while, so the people could stay through September and October, gathering their corn and putting it away. When the charco was all dry, the people would have to move. Up near the mountains, there were springs. Every family had a regular winter home, near some spring and generally the people of a whole village moved together. So each village was really in two places. It had one place in the valley which was called the Fields, because that was where the corn was raised. It had another in the mountains, called the Well. At the Field village, they were all busy working on their crops and gathering wild things. At the Well village they spent their time in hunting.

If we turn to the Pima, we should not find any such movements as this. The Pima lived by a wide river and they dug irrigation ditches for their fields. They hunted in the winter, just as the Papago did, but they did not have to go away and camp for months while they were doing it.

Plate 1. Papago costume: breechclouts, wrap-around skirts and sandals. All wear long hair. Women have tattooed chins.

WHAT DID THEY WEAR?

In such a warm country, the People did not need much clothing. Women wore a one-piece skirt made of a piece of buckskin or some home-woven cotton cloth, twisted around the hips and reaching to the knees. We shall have more to say about this cotton later. It was raised in the Pima country, for the Papago desert was too hot and dry. But the Papago often went to visit the Pima and trade with them, so both River People and Desert People used cotton. Men wore a breechclout of buckskin or cotton. They needed nothing on their feet except when making long journeys and then they wore sandals of mountain sheep skin. Sometimes they wove their sandals out of twisted string. If you have read about the Paiute and the "Mission" Indians, relatives of the People, you will remember that they wore a costume very much like this. It was the regular clothing over a large part of the Southwest and of Mexico.

Plate 2. *Pima sandal of cowhide.

Both men and women among the People had long flowing hair which was considered the chief sign of beauty. They wore earrings of turquoise and other stones, sometimes reaching to their shoulders. Men in those days wore more ornaments then women and the stories often tell of the beautiful long earrings worn by handsome young men.

To cover the upper part of their bodies, they rubbed on grease in cold weather. For special occasions, they used red, yellow, and white paint made from clay. The women in particular, used to paint designs on their bodies showing birds and butterflies and stalks of corn. Women had a permanent discoloration on their faces where they tattooed blue lines from the mouth to the chin. It was a painful process done by picking the lines with a cactus thorn and then rubbing the soot from a greasewood fire. But no woman over sixteen would go without these lines for they felt a face all of one color was "uninteresting." Children wore nothing at all unless their mothers wrapped them in a piece of buckskin or woven cotton.

WHAT DID THEY LIVE IN?

There was very little material in the desert for building houses. In fact, a house was not needed for much except shelter from the rain and for storing property. The People built a dome made of bent rods leaning across four rafters. Over the rods they tied on bundles of brush to shed the rain. On the roof, they piled more brush and over that, earth so that they had

Plate 3. Woman with tattooed face.

a solid, heavy covering to keep out heat and cold. There were no windows. The door was only large enough to crawl through, but that kept out enemies and made it easy to close the house. Generally one family had three or four little round houses like this, one for the parents and others for the married sons who all brought their wives to live at home.

*In former times, the material was mountain sheep skin.

Plate 4. Framework of Papago house: a dome made of bent rods.

Cooking was done outside the house in a circle cleared on the sand and with a fence of brush strung around it to keep out blowing dust. Generally there was only one of these kitchens for three or four houses and the women all brought their food and cooked together. Nearby, they had a storehouse made like the livinghouses but smaller, and here the whole family kept their corn and beans and the wild seeds they

Plate 5. Completed house covered with brush and earth. Canvas in the doorway is a modern touch.

had gathered. For summer living, they made a big arbor with a heavy roof of brush covered with earth and under this they did all their work and eating except in cold and rainy weather.

There was one more building in the family group. This was a small house at a distance with the door facing away from the huts. Here the women of the family went to stay once a month. It was the belief of the People that at such times a magic power descended on women and made them dangerous to everyone around them, but especially to the men and the tools men used. If they touched a man's bow, it would not shoot and if they ate the animal a man had killed, the meat would be poisoned. So the safest thing was for the women to stay away until all danger had passed.

WHAT DID THEY EAT?

The desert country of the Papago looks at first as though no food could be found there, but in the centuries of wandering over hills and valleys, the Indians had found that every cactus has some sort of fruit. The prickly pear they could eat raw after they had scraped off the thorns; the little hard buds of the cholla (pronounced choya) could be eaten after baking in a bed of coals for a night and day; the giant cactus gives a fruit like a fig, out of which they made a drink and a sweet jam. Even the seeds of this cactus could be ground up for flour. The Desert People also found seeds on the summer plants which grew in the rainy season and all of these they ground on their grinding slabs.

There were several kinds of roots which the People ate like potatoes. Then there were green stalks which they could eat raw or roasted in the ashes. The flowering stalks of the century plant and of the yucca are tender when young, and both of these they picked and roasted. It was the woman's duty to gather all of these wild fruits and women went out

Plate 6. Gathering fruit of giant cactus.

15

Plate 7. Man and woman planting corn.

in parties with nets on their backs to carry the load. They camped until they had picked the plants clean, and then they dried the fruit or roasted it before carrying it back. Sometimes they dug pits out in the desert and buried the dried fruit. Later in winter, when the family supply was low, they came and got it.

Besides the wild plants, every family had a little patch in a low spot where they raised corn, beans, and squash. All of these are ancient Indian food cultivated long before the Whites arrived in America. The Papago like other people in the Southwest had corn of different colors: white, blue, red, and black. Besides these they had a mixture of two colors called "laughing corn" and a mixture of all the colors called "crazy corn."

The Pima, of course, raised much more corn than the Papago. In fact, they raised so much that some Papago used to come over and live with them in bad years. The Pima had plenty of beans and squash, too. But they used to go out in the desert and get the wild things, like the Papago. They did not have to go far from their river to find desert country. However, they did not go constantly. They liked the wild things, but only for variety. The never had to live on them for a season, as the Desert People sometimes did.

It was generally the men who planted the fields and cared for them. In Pima country, men went out in the summer when the river was full, cleaned their ditches, and turned the water in. In Papago country, they had to wait until the rain water had stood on the hard earth long enough to soften it. Then they made holes with a sharp stick and dropped in the corn kernels. Often the oldest man of the family spoke to the corn, saying something like this:

"Here I drop you in the earth. Now you will come up like a tall feather headdress. So my children shall eat and they shall eat too—my friends who come from far away."

While the corn was growing, the old man of the family sang to it:

"On Tecalote fields, the corn was growing green, growing green.

I came,

I saw the tassels waving in the wind

And I whistled softly for joy."

Plate 8. Hunter in deerskin disguise.

There were songs when the corn was knee high; songs when the tassels formed; when the ears formed; and when the corn was ripe. There were other songs for the beans and squash.

In the winter, the family moved to the mountains and the men hunted deer. There were plenty of deer in those days. Still, hunters always sang songs to make the animals come to them. Sometimes a number of men got together and surrounded a large space where they thought there were deer. They drove them into an opening in the rocks and there two good marksmen stood with bows and arrows to shoot them down. At other times, a man went alone or with one helper. It was only very skilled hunters who did this and they were called "Headbearers." The reason for the name was that they made a disguise out of a deer head which they pulled over their own heads like a mask. They painted their bodies black in back and white in front and they walked on all fours, imitating the actions of the deer. In this way if they walked against the wind so they could not be smelled, they could come close and shoot the deer while he still thought it was another deer.

It took young boys a long time to learn to be "Headbearers" and only a few were skillful enough to do it. It was a rule that a boy must not eat the first four deer he killed, but must give them to the old man who had taught him. When he had finally learned, he was a rich man for meat was valuable. He gave meat to all his relatives, and the relatives in turn raised corn for him. Sometimes the Headbearers traded venison for cotton. They learned to dress buckskin and dye it red with the juice of a root. Many people came to a hunter to trade baskets of corn and beans or raw cotton for this valuable buckskin and only a few could afford to have skirts or breechclouts made of it.

There were a great many animals to be found in the desert besides deer. Everyone hunted the rabbits: jack rabbits and cottontails. Boys used to go out after them with small bows and arrows and it was their regular duty to keep the family supplied. Besides rabbits, there were ground squirrels which could be poked out of their holes with sticks; rats which could be trapped or shot with arrows; and even tiny mice which would do for meat when nothing else could be found. There were plenty of quail and doves, and all of these small animals the young people shot or trapped.

The way to cook meat was to hold it on a stick over the fire. Small animals could be roasted in the ashes with their fur left on as protection. Sometimes the women of the family made a stew in a clay pot with rabbit meat, roots, and corn.

The People also had smoking tobacco and chewing gum, for both are Indian institutions. They gathered wild tobacco, and a few old men learned to raise it and keep the seeds. They always planted it far from the village for they said the tobacco was shy and would not grow if people looked at it. They dried the leaves and kept them for solemn occasions. Smoking among them was not a mere pleasure. It was an important act which took place at the beginning of a council meeting or when someone was asking the favor of the gods. The People had no pipes but placed their tobacco in pieces of hollow reed, six inches long. At the council meeting there was just one of these and each man took four puffs and passed it to the man on his right, calling him by the term of relationship. When they could not get a reed, they wrapped the tobacco in the white, inner sheath of the corn ear.

For chewing gum, they had the juice of the milkweed vine which hardens if it is heated and allowed to cool. Then there was a sweet gum found on the mesquite tree and another on a little gray leaved bush, the same under which the Coyote was said to have been born.

WHAT DID THEY MAKE?

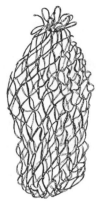

Plate 9. String bag for carrying venison.

One of the first necessities for the People was rope. They used it to tie together the beams of the houses and then to tie on the thatch. They used it, too, to tie up bundles of deer meat and household articles that were to be carried. Men made this sort of tough rope by tearing in two the sword-like leaves of the bear grass or the yucca and tying the two halves together. No one could start to build a house until he had a pile of such tying materials.

But they also made twisted string for finer work. The coarsest sort was made of the fibre of the century plant, which Mexicans call mescal. This plant was good to eat, too, and whole families of Papago made expeditions to mountains near the Mexican border where it grew. They took big

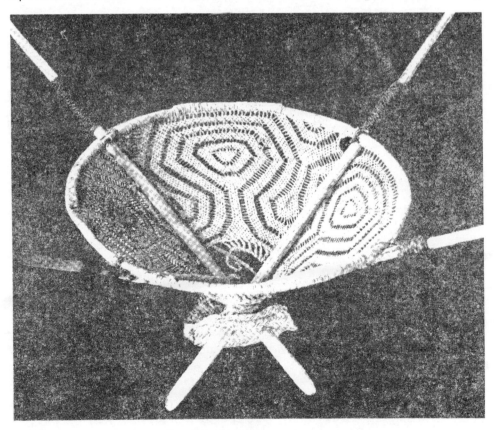

Plate 10. Woman's carrying net.

Plate 11. Pima woman with a load of wood in her carrying net. "Helping stick" on which she leans when rising stands at front of load.

loads of it to trade with the Pima. When they were gathering mescal, they camped for days on the job. First they cut off the leaves with a stone knife and roasted the cabbage-like heads in a huge pit, warmed at the bottom with hot stones. The heads, after roasting all night, were like huge artichokes, with a sweet, slimy taste. The cord they made out of the green ends of the leaves which had been cut off. First, they pounded out the fibre with a stone. Then a man twisted it into string by rolling it up and down on the bare leg with the palm of the hand. String-making is man's work among many Indian tribes, but the Papago men did more with it than most. They made a rough string bag with wide meshes in which they carried their deer meat and burdens while traveling.

Women used the same string to make their own carrying baskets and these were of an interesting sort not found anywhere else north of Mexico. They were in cone shape made with a stitch like crochet. They were attached on the top to a ring of bent wood about two feet across and kept in shape by four upright sticks: two long ones which lay across the women's backs and two short ones in front. The cone shaped net in its stick frame could stand alone while the woman loaded it with wood or water jars or vegetables. The story is that once these carrying nets walked on their four legs but that the coyote, who is always the mischief-maker in Papago stories, laughed at them so they became angry and declared that ever after the women would have to carry them.

Women were very proud of their carrying nets and made the crochet work in beautiful patterns which they dyed blue with soot and red with clay. In olden days, no woman went out without her carrying net. She ran at a jog trot and she declared that the load on her back pushed her on. Old women now say it is hard to walk without the load, but the young women laughingly call the cars which their husbands buy their "carrying nets."

The mescal string was tough and bulky and sometimes a finer, stronger string was needed. For this the Papago used their own long, black hair, particularly that of

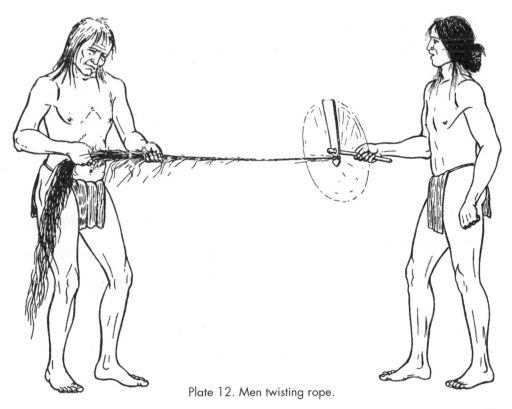

Plate 12. Men twisting rope.

the women which was cut off at the neck in mourning. When the Papago were given horses by the Spaniards, they used horsehair in the same way.

Men made hair rope, just as they did all other string making but they used a very clever tool, which they seem to have learned from the ancient Spaniards. This was a slab of wood attached to an upright stick so that it could be whirled around. One end of the fibres was attached to a knob on the slab while a helper held the other end. Then the rope-maker whirled the slab and the fibres twisted. Papago men may still be seen at this task, making the ropes of horsehair which they use for bridles.

They made fastenings, too, of long strips of buckskin. With these they fastened together their baby carriers, their traps for birds and rats, and the doors of their houses which were made of light sticks bound together. For very fine work, they used deer sinew and every man kept a bundle of it stuck in the thatch of his roof.

Plate 13.
Spindle.

The Papago, unlike most desert Indians, made cotton string and cloth. Generally, they got their cotton from the Pima. They often went over to visit their cousins on the river, especially in winter when there was nothing much to do. They took deer skins and cactus seeds and mescal fibre and brought back things which grew in the wet country, like willow for baskets and cotton for string. But they managed to raise a little cotton, too. Only a few old men had fields of it and these were very small, but cotton was valuable and people who did not raise it came to trade for it with corn and beans and deer meat. The old men twisted the cotton into string with a spindle, a slender stick with a slab on the end to make it whirl. They held this slab between their toes and twisted the fibres around the spindle sticks as people used to do in Bible times. Then they wove the cotton into strips of cloth long enough for a woman's skirt or a sheet.

There were only two or three weavers in all the country although the Pima, who had better land for cotton growing, wove much more. A weaver would make himself a simple loom out of the smooth rods which grow inside the giant cactus and are called the "cactus ribs." He made a square frame of four of these, tied together with string and placed on short stakes driven into the ground so that it looked like a bed frame. When he needed cotton yarn enough to weave a piece of cloth, he got all his friends to spend some hours spinning. Since they were busy in the day time, they used to spin at night while keeping awake and watching for the enemy. After two or three nights, there might be enough for a skirt and the old man squatted by his loom

Plate 14. Pima loom. Model in picture is not supported on stakes as was usual practice.

and wove for several days. The weave was perfectly plain except that sometimes he put in a few threads at the border which were dyed red with the root of a plant.

Women almost never wove although old women sometimes helped with the spinning. Woman's chief work was basketry for the Papago moved about so much they could not afford to have heavy breakable pots. They used baskets to store food; to hold water; to roast corn by shaking it with hot embers; to serve food. They even turned baskets upside down and used them as drums. Every girl learned to make

23

baskets from her childhood up but generally the young women were busy doing the heavy work of searching for wood and water and grinding corn, so it was the older women who sat under the shelter, twisting willow strands for baskets.

Plate 15. Basketry awl with wooden handle.

Willow was the best material for basketry. But the tree grows only near water so there was not much of it in the Papago country. The Papago used to trade for it when they went on visits to the Pima, or simply made long trips to get it. Later, they have found that the soft white blades which grow at the center of the yucca plant make very pretty baskets and these are now used for trade. The baskets of the People are always black and white. The white is willow with the Pima, willow or yucca with the Papago. The black comes from the pod of a long bean called Devils Claw. Devils Claw grows wild but it is so valuable for basketry that a woman who found the plant often made a little fence around it to keep away gophers and rabbits. Many woman saved the seeds and cultivated a patch of it in their gardens.

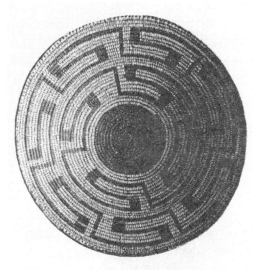

The People's baskets are made by coiling, which has been explained in the paper on the Paiute. It is a form of sewing in which some rough foundation is twisted round spirally to form the frame of the basket. The rounds of the frame are sewed together with flexible shoots which cover them entirely so that only this sewed part shows. Women of the People did their sewing with a cactus thorn or a small sharp stick which they poked into the basket frame, like an awl. This made a hole big enough so that the willow shoot could be pushed through. Baskets made of willow and Devils Claw were very strong and if they were

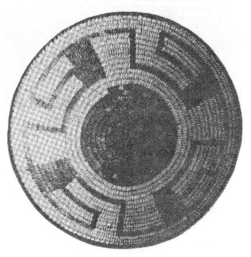

Plate 16. Basket bowls of willow and devil's claw.

24

Plate 17. Large storage basket of bark and straw.

wet, they swelled so much that they were water tight. The yucca which is now used does not become water tight but baskets made from it are only for trade. The Pima made a specially large coiled basket in which they stored their grain. It was so large that the woman who was coiling it had to stand inside. It was made of straw sewed together with bark and, after the Pima had learned to use wheat, the straw was generally wheat straw. The picture on this page shows the coiling stitches very plainly.

There was another form of basketry much older than the willow bowls and dishes. This was a sort of weaving like a kindergarten mat. Women would pick the long straight leaves of bear grass, a kind of yucca which grows from the ground in huge heads, like a palm tree without any trunk. They pushed off the leaves with a long stick which was flat and sharp at the end like a chisel. Then they peeled the leaves and split them with hands and teeth until they had straight, stiff strands, half an inch or an inch wide and three or four feet long.

Plate 18. Section of beargrass mat, showing method of weaving.

It was hard work to weave these strands into a square mat but they used no loom. The woman simply sat on the ground and added new strands first on one side of the mat and then the other as the square kept growing. These mats were hard and

Plate 19. Beargrass mat, used for seats or bedding.

stiff but in the old days, they were the only thing which could be used for bedding. Every house had a row of such mats around the edge to be used as mattresses. The father and mother slept on one and the children on the others, two and two. In the daytime, the mats could be taken outdoors and used by the women to sit on while they worked at their basketry. The way to receive a guest was always to pull out a mat for him.

Plate 20. Ancient form of basket used for scalps, feathers, and other sacred things.

This mat form of weaving was used to make a very old kind of basket, looking like some of the straw suitcases we have now. It consisted of two straw boxes which fitted one over the other like a lid. This kind of basketry was used for keeping very sacred things—either the eagle feathers that belonged to the town and were hung up in its ceremonials or perhaps a scalp which a warrior had taken. The same technique was used to make head rings of basketry on which women rested pots when they carried them on their heads. (See plate 37.)

Plate 21. Modern Pima woman making pots with completed water jar beside her.

Plate 22. Girl preparing tortillas.

Besides their baskets, a few women could make pots and these they traded with other women for baskets and vegetables. You have noticed already that the Papago were quite used to trading. One pot that every family needed was the big water jar, three feet high, made out of coarse clay which let the air through so that water kept cool by evaporation. This was a very clever idea for in that warm country water in the summer time was actually hot, and the only way to keep it cool enough to drink was to stand the drinking jar in the shade where a breeze was blowing so that the water would evaporate.

Besides the drinking jar, women made nicely painted vessels for storing seeds and also rough pots for cooking. (See plate 44.) One of these was a sort of griddle, shaped like a large round plate made as smooth as possible. The women placed it on the coals and let it get very hot, then she took a ball of cornmeal batter and patted it between her hands until it was as thick as a pancake. She dropped this on the hot griddle for a minute, turned it with her fingers and then took it off. This was the tortilla made by so many Mexican tribes and was the regular Papago bread.

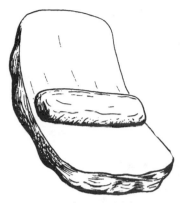

Plate 23. Metate with muller.

The men made all the stone tools that were needed. They looked in the mountains for slabs of lava or granite which would make good grinding stones for their wives. A grinding stone was a rough oblong about one and one-half feet long and perhaps six inches thick. If the surface was not rough enough, the man sometimes hacked it with a hard stone. For a grinder, he got a cylindrical stone which had been rolled about by water until its surface was smooth. This slab and grinder were cherished possessions in every family. They were too heavy to carry about so the woman had one at each dwelling place and when she was away, she buried it for safety. At old villages of the People, these buried stones can still be found and sometimes women go looking for them rather than make a new one.

The man was very busy making bows and arrows because the People shot all their game rather than catching it in nets as so many Indians did. The man had to hunt through the mountains for stone for arrow points. Then he must pick the stalks of the soap weed, at a time of the year when they were green for of these he made his arrow shafts. He used a little stick of hard wood at the end of the shaft to which he could tie the point. For this tying, he needed plenty of deer sinew which he kept rolled in little balls and stuck into the house thatch.

For arrow feathers, he could use turkey and crow tails if he were only hunting, but for war he must have eagle feathers because the turkey is not brave. When he had collected all these things, he generally called a number of neighbors and an old man who knew the special songs for arrow-making. If all of them worked all day, they could make a hundred arrows and their host would feed them while working. When later, one of the guests needed arrows, the first man would help with the work and so return the favor. His bow he would make out of box thorn or mulberry. He cut the wood when it was full of sap; shaped it with a stone knife so that it was thick in the middle and slender at both ends. Then he laid it in the ashes, bent into the proper shape with stones to hold it. He made two bow strings out of the sinew of a deer's back and kept an extra one always ready.

Plate 24. Basketry cradle board. When used, a mat of buckskin or willowbark covered this frame.

Plate 25. Starting fire by twirling stick of hardwood, its point placed in hole in piece of soft wood.

There were two or three household tools made of wood. The People had a very useful material in the smooth long ribs which they found inside the giant cactus when the pulp outside had rotted away. They used these long slats to make a pair of tongs with which to pick the thorny fruit of the prickly pear. They tied two of them together to make a very long pole with a tiny crosspiece at the top and with this they hooked down the fruit of the giant cactus. (See plate 6.) Out of cactus rib, too, they made the long bar with holes in it in which they twirled a stick of hardwood in order to start a fire. Cactus rib was used for the spindle on which they spun cotton, and for the twister to make hair rope. (See plates 12 and 13.)

Cactus rib, too, formed part of the baby's cradle board. This might, really, be called a basket, for it was an oval frame of elastic willow wood, with cactus slats tied across it. Then there was a mat of soft cedar bark for the baby to lie on and a little awning, woven as the bear grass mats were woven, to shade his eyes.

They also made musical instruments for their songs and dances for these were the religious ceremonies that made up the most important parts of their life. For their

Plate 26. Notched stick, a musical instrument.

most solemn ceremonies of all, they used a kind of drum, which was nothing more than a bowl-shaped basket turned upside down. Against it, they rested one end of a long stick, carved with notches for the whole of its length. Then another stick was rubbed up and down the notches, making an exciting rattling sound such as is often heard in modern bands. Sometimes they merely tapped one stick on the basket.

For some ceremonies, like the rain singing and the girl's dance, they always used a rattle. It was made of a hollow gourd, with a wooden handle attached and with small pebbles inside to make the rattling. This was the instrument used by the medicine man in curing the sick. They made a flute out of a long reed and many are the stories of boys who played this flute to attract the girls. They learned from the Yaquis to make a special kind of rattle which was used at the Easter dance. This was a long string of little white cocoons, filled with gravel, which a dancer twisted around his legs so that they rattled when he danced.

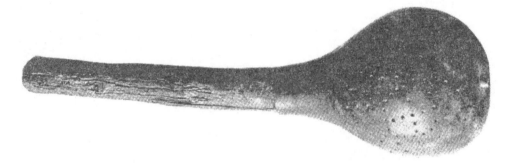

Plate 27. Rattle made of hollow gourd, with small pebbles inside.

LIFE IN THE VILLAGE

GOVERNMENT:

THE PEOPLE were divided roughly into two halves. The Papago called them Coyote People and Buzzard People. The Pima sometimes called them Red Ants and White Ants. Many Indians make this sort of division, but with the People it did not figure much. The two halves used to laugh at each other. The Buzzards would call the Coyotes tricky, then the Coyotes would say that the Buzzard was a coward and ate the game which other animals had killed. Sometimes in ceremonies, half of the dancers had to be Coyote and half Buzzard, but as a usual thing the division did not matter.

There was another division more important and this was the separation into clans. A clan in this case meant a man and all his descendants through his sons. Women belonged to the clans of their fathers but when they married, their children of course went with their fathers and not their mothers. There were four clans, or some say five, though the fifth was not very distinct. The clan names cannot be translated: "Apap," "Apki," "Mam," "Vaf," and "Okari." None of the people could ever forget his clan because when he spoke to his father, instead of calling him father, he called him by his clan name. That meant that he would say to his father "my Apap." To his father's sister, he would say "my Apap Old Woman," and to his father's older brother "my Apap Old Man." So the People all knew their clans but they did not think about them much. What they really thought about was the village.

Most of the people in the villages were relatives: generally on the father's side. They elected a headman who was a sort of judge and shepherd to the people. He settled quarrels and told them when to have ceremonies. He lived in the house where they had their meeting which was just like a dwelling house only larger. Later he did not live in the meeting house but in a smaller house beside it. At night, he built a fire in the house and standing on the roof of his shelter, he called to the men to come and discuss village affairs. Sometimes he had a messenger or two who were called his "legs" and if he did not have a strong voice, he could appoint a man to call out the announcements from the roof top. This man was called his "voice."

It was the business of the headman to keep the sacred things that belonged to the village. Sometime there was a string of eagle feathers which could produce rain, or there might be a magic stone or a little carved image. These were in the big square

Plate 28. Council meeting.

basket which has been described and he kept them either in the council house or out in the desert among the rocks where they would be safe from the enemy. He had to know the magic speeches which were recited to bring rain and to chase away disease, and he had to preside at ceremonies. Before this headman died, he generally chose one of his young relatives: a son or nephew or perhaps a younger brother and to him he taught the speeches and the care of the sacred things. After he was gone, the village probably chose this young man to take up the work but if they did not approve, they asked him to teach someone else.

Most villages had a man to lead in war, whom they used to call the "hard man" or the "bitter man." He was chosen because he was brave and would not give in to the enemy. He, too, had to know certain speeches which were magic and would take away the enemy's power. He passed his office to a younger man just as the village "headman" did and if he grew too old to lead, he still recited the speeches while the younger man did the fighting.

Then there was a hunt leader who directed the hunts for deer and rabbits. He also must recite speeches which made the animals come to be killed. Sometimes this same man was the leader for games. The People were great racers and kickball players and often one village challenged another. They needed a man to train their young men in athletics and take charge of the betting; but he also must make a magic speech. Both the hunt and game leaders passed on their duties as the headman did.

All these officers were almost priests. Their duties were as much to make the magic speeches as to direct the people. They really had no authority and the people took their advice only because they respected them. It was all the men of the village who made the decisions. Every night, especially in the summer when all were camped together, the men came together in the council house. There the headman often made them a speech, going over the duties which he thought all should perform. He told them to work hard and always to be ready with their bow and arrows in case their enemies should come. Then he brought up any special business and asked the advice of everyone. They never took action unless all the men agreed. That is to say, the older men. Young men until they were past thirty rarely spoke in meeting. They sat at the back of the house listening and if war was decided upon, they did the fighting but they were not thought wise enough to speak until they had experience.

This was the way it was in very ancient times, according to the old men. But the People began to know White men about two hundred and fifty years ago. Then their government changed a little. The Spaniards were the first White people they met and the Spaniards were used to having a mayor in every town or a governor in every state. They were not used to waiting while a council decided things. They thought every Indian town ought to have one man who would tell the Spaniards just what the Indians would do. They could give orders to this man and he could give them to the people. So they appointed a man of that sort in every town of the people and they called him governor. (In Spanish, the word is gobernador.) The People could not say it very well, for they have no R in their language. They said gobenal and they say it still. The governor whom the Spaniards appointed was generally the old headman. Sometimes however, he was not. There are some Papago towns now which have a headman for the ceremonies and a governor too. Some have no headman but just a governor.

WAR:

The People did not really like to go to war. They were too busy cultivating their fields and hunting for food to care to go out fighting. But the fierce Apaches who lived in the mountains near them often attacked their villages and carried off horses, women and children. So the People had to fight and they did well at it. They had fairly good weapons. Most of the men carried bows, with something like a hundred stone tipped arrows. A few, however, carried small leather shields and clubs made of hard wood. Some of these clubs looked exactly like the potato mashers to be seen in modern kitchens and they were very good for cracking enemy heads. Men who used them had to get much closer to the enemy than the bowmen did so they had to be specially brave. But the bowmen, too, sometimes carried clubs so as to finish off the enemies they had wounded.

Plate 29. War club and shield.

In spite of the equipment, the People felt success in war depended almost as much on magic as on bravery. Before they went out, they had a number of magical recitations made by the War Leader and describing the triumph which they wished to have. They felt that if this were described in magic words, it would surely come about. When they camped in the hills on the night before they marched against the enemy, they sang almost all night.

Their songs told how the enemy was conquered; how his shield fell to pieces and his club was useless.

When it came to actual fighting, there was a good deal of difference between the Papago and the Pima. The Pima, it is said, often got together quite a big army. They marched to the place where they were to fight, and talked to the war chief on the opposite side, calling him names. Sometimes the whole army shouted at the other army, calling them cowards and women.

Perhaps the River People learned that way of doing from some of their neighbors, like the Yuma. The Desert People, however, were too busy for that elaborate kind of war. They took only a few men, perhaps ten or twelve and they went to the enemy's country and came back as fast as they could. They never let the enemy know they were coming. They rushed on a village at dawn, took a few scalps and hurried away. As soon as a man had killed an enemy, he ceased fighting. This contact with death was thought to bring him under magic power and he must be purified as will be explained later. So he blackened his face and stood outside the conflict. When the leader saw that two or three men had retired like this, he ended the fight. Then the victorious party marched home.

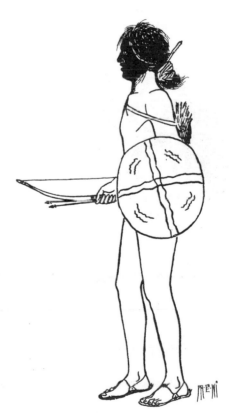

Plate 30. Enemy killer with his face blackened.

The killers did not go with them for though they were the real heroes of the occasions, they must spend sixteen days purifying themselves from the strange magic which had touched them. They marched behind the rest of the party, eating very little and painting their faces black. The main party tried to camp so that they could enter the home village at dawn. From their camp they sent a fast runner to shout the news of victory and to mention the names of the killers. The wives of these heroes must then go away from the rest of the village and purify themselves by fasting just as their husbands did. This was a very different idea from that held by many Indians whose main ambition in life was to get war honors.

Plate 31. Old woman dancing with scalp.

With the Papago, the killer had done a public duty, perhaps against his will, but instead of honor, he had what almost seemed a punishment. His reward was in knowing that he had helped his village and that in the end he would have the power and respect of one who had gone through a long purification. It was the men who had done no killing who received all the honor. They marched into the village, carrying the scalps on a pole. They were met by the old women who seized the scalps and danced with them. Among the Papago, young women were shy but it was the old women who ventured to dance and sing in public. The party went to the council house where the warriors told the story of their expedition to the whole village. Then they placed the scalp on its pole in the dance ground and men, women, and children danced around it. None touched it for the scalp had evil power. For sixteen nights they danced every night, singing the ancient songs which Elder Brother, Itoi, had composed when he first conquered the country.

All this time, the killers were sitting alone in the desert waiting until the magic power should be tamed and they could join the others. It was only when the sixteen days were passed that they came to the dance ground. They brought in with them their weapons which were still thought to be dangerous. To make the weapons safe again, different men danced with them in a wild dramatic war dance while old men sang. The former warriors smoked over the killers and sang to them and at last brought them back to human companionship. After this, each kept the scalp he had taken. He had a special basket made for it and there he kept it, wrapped in eagle feathers. He gave it food now and then and cane cigarettes and he spoke to it as though it were a friend or child. The idea was that the scalp had now been adopted into his family and that all its strange power would be used up to help him. Warriors who had such scalps were the most reverenced people in the community and there was no power quite so great as "scalp power."

GAMES:

In winter, when most of the food gathering was over, the Papago had plenty of time for games. All young men practiced kickball with a ball about the size of a croquet ball, sometimes made of stone covered with gum and sometimes hacked out of wood. The man kicked this by putting his toe under it and lifting it. Some old men who played this game barefooted during all their youth now have toe nails as thick as horn. Men said they could run more easily with a ball than without it and they used to cover twenty or thirty miles a day. Sometimes three or four men ran together, each one kicking the ball as he came up to it.

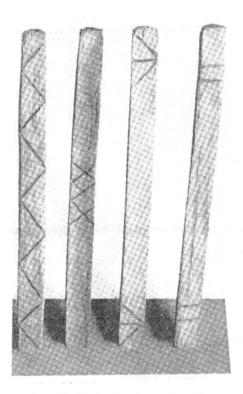

Plate 32. Marked sticks used as dice.

They also practiced racing on a track, a half or quarter mile long, which was cleared on the sand outside the village. The relay race was a favorite game. Any number of men ran on each side. At each end stood a starter and in the middle of the track two men with marking sticks. They placed the sticks at the point where the man from opposite sides passed— one toward each end. As one side gained, the two sticks moved nearer to-gether and when the sticks met, the race

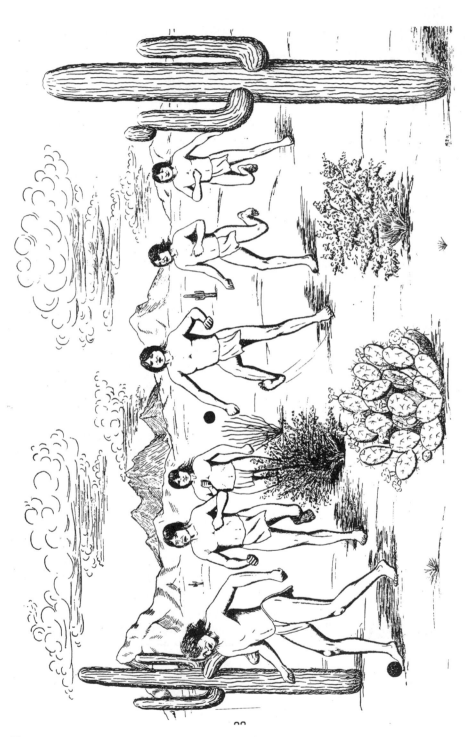

Plate 33. Men playing kickball.

Plate 34. Men playing hidden ball. One side has hidden a wild bean in one of four marked sections of reed lying on ground. The other side is guessing where it is.

was over. Women used to race, too, and they also played a game like shinny in which they used as a ball two short pieces of mesquite root tied together with string. The stick was a long slender wand slightly curved at one end.

Another favorite game was something like *parchese* on a large scale. A great square of stones was made on the ground with the corners marked out. Four men played; two started at one corner and two at the opposite one. Each had a pebble which he moved according to the throw of some dice. These were flat sticks painted on one side with different designs. They had names such as "old man" and "old woman." They were tapped on stone and thrown on the ground and from the way they fell a man knew how he might move his pebble. The game was to get around the whole square and "home." Another game was to hide a wild bean in one of four piles of sand and guess where it was. A number of men played on each side but one did the hiding for each side and one the guessing. Most of the village watched and bet on the result.

Women had a dice game played with four sticks—black on one side and white on the other. It counted two if they fell on white and four it they were all black, otherwise nothing. "We used to play all the afternoon when we were through our work," said one old woman, "and then if we didn't like the result we would finish with a race."

There was one game which women and children both liked. It is popular with many American Indians and even with modern children who sometime call it "diavolo." It is played with a number of rings, strung on a string with a stick fastened at the end

41

Plate 35. Rings of squash rind used in a game.

of it. The game is to throw the rings up in the air and then catch as many as possible on the point of the stick. Indians made the rings of all sorts of material but the Pima and Papago, who were farmers, made them of squash rind. They cut out the center of a squash when it was soft and sliced the shell crosswise, forming a number of rings of different sizes. They pressed these under something until they were hard and flat as leather. All they had to do then was to provide the string and the stick, as any modern school children could do. They scored in this game by moving beans or pebbles along the spiral decorations of a flat basket.

TRADE:

We have already noticed things which the People traded among themselves. The hunter sold deer meat and dressed buckskin to people who came with baskets of vegetables or with cotton cloth. The weaver sold his cloth and the woman pottery maker sold her pots. Of course there was no money but people had a pretty good idea what a basket of dried beans or corn was worth and the amount of meat or cotton given in exchange for it was always about the same.

42

The Papago were specially fond of traveling to trade. They used to make journeys over the river country where the Pima lived and down into Mexico where there were other Pima and Papago. They took with them the specialties of their desert country; syrup and jam from the giant cactus, or the heavy woven mats of beargrass. They brought back vegetables and basketry material. More than that, they brought the things which these cousins of theirs had traded from the white man. In that way the Papago first got Spanish clothes, knives, beads, and guns.

Sometimes they brought nothing with them to trade but their own labor. They used to go, in the spring, to these relatives in the river valleys and plant their crops, getting, as pay, their daily food. Again, they would go in the fall to harvest and many of them still go, in this way, to take care of the Pima wheat. "We are not lazy people," they always say. "When there is no water in our own land, we go to work somewhere else."

LEARNING:

The People taught their children to count up to ten, using words that had to do with ten fingers. They have now words for the numbers up to a hundred and even one for a thousand but these they seem to have got from the Spaniards. Before white men came, they did not need to count so high. They measured quantity by the black marks on their baskets and length by the width of a hand, of an arm to the elbow or of a whole arm. When they wanted to remind themselves of the number of days before a feast or before going to war, they cut a number of sticks and stood them in a row. Each day they knocked one down and when all were lying flat, the expected day had come.

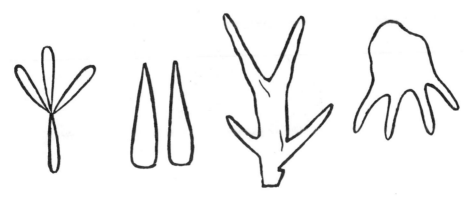

Plate 36. Typical markings from the Pima calendar stick.

43

They had no writing but still they had a kind of history. This was a long stick, made of a cactus rib, with marks to remind them of the things which had happened every day. The marks were not real writing, for the old man who kept the stick made them up to suit himself. But he remembered what each one meant. Sitting with the stick in his hand, he could lay his thumb on mark after mark and recite the history of his village for eighty years or so. Each village may once have had a stick and now there are at least two. The Pima once had five. None of them go back earlier than 1833 which was "the year the stars fell," and is when there were meteors in Arizona. The sticks may have been begun in that year, though we do not know how. They have been kept up faithfully until a short time ago.

The Papago had names for the chief constellations, including what the Whites call Orion's belt, which they named the Mountain Sheep, the Antelope and the Deer. They also thought of the stars in groups different from those the Whites use. One was the Cactus Stick and one the hand of Elder Brother, who once held up the sky to keep his people from being crushed. They calculated the time for planting, harvesting, and feasts by the positions of the Pleiades which they called the Seven Travelers. They knew that the North Star did not change its position and they called it the Unmoving Star.

They knew something about the value of herbs as medicine. Serious illnesses were treated by the medicine man who did not give medicine but simply sang. Less important ailments like colds and indigestion were treated by the woman of the family who gathered green things while out searching for food. She knew, for instance, that the leaves of the creosote bush, which grows so plentifully in the desert are good for colds and to make a hot vapor bath for rheumatism. She knew that broomweed makes a medicinal tea and she washed sore eyes with a brew of a seed like flax.

Plate 37. Ring of basketry, used by a woman in carrying a pot on her head.

LIFE IN THE FAMILY

BIRTH:

WHEN a Papago child was to be born, both its mother and father were careful not to do anything that would bring bad luck. The father did not go to war or even hunting, because he must not kill at such a time. If he did fight, he would have no strength and he might be killed himself. Just before the baby was to arrive, the mother went to the separate house for women because it was thought dangerous to have such a strange thing as birth take place in the family home. She stayed in the separate hut for a month with her women relatives to look after her. When the moon had gone around "to where it was before," she took her baby to the medicine man for a kind of baptism.

Her husband went with her and the ceremony took place just at sunrise. The medicine man mixed yellow clay in a bowl and with it he marked both the mother and the baby. Then he gave some of the clay to the father, mother and child to eat, singing all the time. This took the strangeness of birth away from the mother and child and made it possible for them to go back and live with other people. The medicine man gave the baby a name which was something magic out of the dreams he had had. These names were often very beautiful like "Dawn Murmur" for a girl, or "Rushing Wind" for a boy. The names were thought to possess magic power and the people did not use them in later life. When they spoke to each other, they used terms of relationship such as "my young brother," "my older sister's child." As the children grew older, they were given nicknames and these could be freely used.

YOUTH:

The baby spent the first year of his life tied to the cradle board. In this way his active young mother could take him with her while she went to fetch wood and water. She placed the board against a tree while she was working and, when she was ready to go home, piled it on top of her load. Almost as soon as he could toddle, he began to follow his father or mother about and try to do anything that they did. By eight or nine years old, if the child was a boy, he was out with bow and arrow, learning to shoot rabbits. If it was a girl, she was stirring the cookpot while her mother went after water and her grandmother taught her housekeeping.

It was the grandparents who did most of the child training for the young parents were busy with the hard work of the family. In the evening, as the family lay on their mats around the fire, the grandfather would talk, telling stories and also teaching the children how they must behave. An even better time for this teaching was in the early morning while it was still dark. Then he would begin talking in a low gentle voice, telling them how they must always work, they must never be idle because it was only by work that people kept alive. The boys, he said, must go out early in the morning and practice running. Running was very important with the Desert People for they needed it in hunting, and the wide empty desert was almost a natural race track. The boys must run until they were exhausted; then as they lay resting on the ground they might have a vision in which some animal could come to them. Animals, the grandfather said, had magic power because they understood how to get their food and how to escape from enemies much better than man. Also they knew magic songs which would cure disease. An animal might sing to the boy and then he must learn the song. Perhaps it would make him a great runner or a great hunter and it would help to cure disease. Whatever it did, it would be his most precious possession all through life. Girls were not expected to have visions like this. But the girls, the old man said, must always work because no one would want a lazy woman for a wife. They must be sure that their men had cool water to drink, and then that they had enough to eat so that they could be strong to fight the enemy. This sort of speech was recited every morning beginning while the children were still too young to understand. When they grew up, they had its teachings firmly in mind.

Children worked during the day but their parents were very careful not to let them get too tired. Besides the regular work, the old men gave the boys practice for war by teaching them to jump and avoid arrows and to shoot at a mark. All young boys in a village practiced racing and boys, and girls too, began when they were tiny. There was a cleared space on the desert outside the village and as soon as they were free from work, the children went there and practiced running with their older relatives to cheer them and give instructions.

When the girls were about fourteen, they had a special ceremony. The Papago felt that everything connected with childbearing was so mysterious that it had a dangerous magic. When the girl became old enough for childbearing, they thought that she must be purified. Otherwise the strange power which had come upon her might harm her, as well as her family. She was sent away into the women's hut for four days with an older woman to teach her. This older woman told her how she must be hard-working in order to get a good husband. Then she gave the girl practice in carrying wood and water which would be her chief duties in life. When the four days were over, a dance was held for the whole village.

These dances were the gayest occasions in Papago life and everyone came from miles around. There was a special singer who knew the songs for girls at such a time. He held his rattle in his right hand and placed his left arm over the girl's shoulder. Then, in a line beyond them, came half the young men and girls in the village with their arms over each other's shoulders. The other half formed a line opposite them. The two lines danced back and forth toward each other all night, singing songs about butterflies and mountains and magic things which brought good luck to the girl. Sometimes they did this every night for a month. That was only if the girl's family could provide food enough, for the whole party had to have a meal at midnight.

No wonder the girl was tired when the month was over! She danced every night and she had to work hard during the day. The idea was that this was a special time in her life which would influence all the future. If she worked hard now, she would always be industrious; if she kept from gossiping now, she would never gossip in the future. So she did her best to insure good luck for ever after. When the month was over, she went to the medicine man who marked her with yellow clay just as he marked a woman who had had a baby. After this, she was a grown woman and her parents could choose a husband for her.

MARRIAGE:

The parents took entire charge of the marriage of their sons and daughters. There was a reason for it for two families united by marriage would always take special care of each other's welfare. It was the girl's parents who did the choosing and they had probably been looking some years for an industrious young man. They chose him from another village since people in their own village were so often relatives. It was not considered right to marry a relative on either the father's or mother's side. If they had a daughter already married, they often gave the younger sister to the same husband for the People had no law against marrying more than one wife. They felt that if the man were industrious, a girl would be better off with him and in her sister's company than with some new man.

They went to the boy's relatives or to the man himself if he had already married one of their daughters, and proposed the marriage. Often they did not tell the girl anything about it until the last moment for she was young and not thought to be wise enough to choose for herself. When the time for the wedding arrived, the man came to the girl's house and stayed four nights. This was the only marriage ceremony. She received a husband while under her mother's care and if all seemed well, he took her back to his home to live. She and her husband lived in the same house with his

47

parents for they were still so young that they were considered like children. The boy was under the father's direction and the girl took her place with his sisters working under the mother-in-law. When they had several children of their own and were at last considered grown up, they built a little round house near the parents. The boy still worked in his father's fields with his father and brothers. The girl and her sisters-in-law took turns with the family cooking.

If a couple did not want to stay together, they could be divorced by merely deciding to separate. The woman went back to her father's house where her man relatives soon found her another husband. Since a woman did at least half of the work of supporting a family, she never need lack a mate. If she had small children, she took them with her. Older ones, especially boys, might stay with the father. If her husband died, she expected one of his younger brothers to marry her and take care of her. This was because the husband's family and the wife's family did not want to separate. If the husband had no brother, they would get one of his cousins to marry the widow. In the same way, if a woman died, her husband would expect her family to give him one of her younger sisters or cousins as a wife.

DEATH:

The People had a feeling that death is dangerous to the remaining members of the family for the dead person is lonely and will try to take them with him if he can. Therefore, they buried the dead person as quickly as possible and though they loved him, they tried not to think of him. Their earliest form of burial was simply to place the body in some opening in the rocks and pile stones above it. Later, they built a sort of stone with a roof over it. Inside they placed the body, sitting up, and they placed with it the weapons or tools that had been used in life. Sometimes they placed a little food there too, for their belief was that the soul took four days to go to the land of the dead and would need food on the journey. The land of the dead was at the East where the rain comes from and was a pleasant, moist land with plenty of food.

As soon as the body had been removed, they burned down the house so that the dead person would not return to it. The relatives cut their hair and the widow or widower did not marry for a year.

LIFE AND THE GODS

THE SACRED STORY:

THE PEOPLE had a long story explaining the beginnings of their world. Every important village had an old man who knew this story and who told it in the winter time. It was thought bad luck to tell it in summer when the stinging creatures were out for they would bite the storyteller or they would send the rain when it was not wanted. The story was in prose and every old man had his own way of telling it, imitating the voices of the characters and giving illustrations of the way every action took place. But at each interesting point, there was a song. These songs were thought to have magic power and whenever the people were in difficulties, just as those first people had been, they sang the songs again and again and got help.

The story tells how, in the beginning, Earthmaker made the whole world out of a little ball of dirt. He danced on it until it spread and touched the edges of the sky. Then there was a great noise and out sprang another being whose name was Itoi, (pronounced Eetoy). Itoi and Earthmaker together put the world in shape. The Coyote, who had been in the world from the beginning, helped them. People came into the world too but they were not the right kind so the two gods decided to destroy them with a flood. They did so and they and Coyote agreed that when the waters went down, whichever of them came out first from hiding should be elder brother.

It was Itoi who gained this title and who has been Elder Brother to the People ever since. He made new people out of clay and taught them all the things they now do. Earthmaker was angry that Itoi had got ahead of him so he sank through the earth and disappeared. Itoi lived with his people a long time and helped them in all their troubles. But at last he changed his nature, so the people quarreled with him and killed him. These people, says the story, were not the Papago and Pima. They were the people who formerly lived in the land and who built the ruins of Casa Grande.

Itoi was angry at them and he went under the earth, looking for friends who would come and help him drive them away. Under the earth he found the Papago and Pima for they, like many Indians in the Southwest, believe that they came from underground. He led them through the country and they drove out those who lived there, leaving only the ruins which can be seen today. Then he told them to settle just where they are now, and he showed them the feast they must hold to bring the rain and to keep the world in happiness.

Plate 38. Rain Dance. Dancers have decorated their bodies for the occasion with painted patterns.

The People say that, in former times, the religion of the Pima and Papago was just the same and they all had the same ceremonies. However, the Pima began giving up the ceremonies almost seventy-five years ago and it would be hard to find any of them in Pima country now. So, at this point, we must leave the River People aside and tell about the ceremonies of the Desert People.

RAINMAKING:

These ceremonies were all connected, somehow, with getting rain and food. Since there was no running water in the land and lack of rain would mean starvation, rainmaking ceremonies were the most important of all. These came in July, just before the rainy season began, and they were considered the beginning of the Papago year. To make rain magic, the Papago make a liquor from the fruit of the giant cactus. The liquor was brewed with singing and ceremony and the men drank it, filling themselves with moisture as they wished the earth to be filled.

The giant cactus grows in tall columns, sometimes twenty or thirty feet high, and bears on its top a cluster of fruits. Every family still has a special camp in some cactus grove where they go for the three weeks in late June and in early July when the fruit is ripe. The women of the family go out in the morning and evening and hook down the fruits with their long poles, carrying them home in huge baskets. In the hot part of the day, they cook the fruit over a fire since it would spoil immediately in the heat. Then they strain the juice out through a loosely woven basket and keep it in a sealed jar. When every family has a jar or two of juice, they go back to the summer village where the ceremony takes place.

The headman of the village, or someone else who had this special duty, receives the juice from all the different families and mixes it with water in several large jars in the council house. It is left there for two nights to ferment and while it is fermenting, the people outside sing songs about the rain which it will bring. A small fire is made and the magic eagle feathers are strung up. Then the people form a circle around the fire, men and women holding hands, with the song leader and his rattle at the head. At the end of the second night, the headman announces that the liquor is ready and that the people shall come in the morning to drink.

This drinking is not a matter of pleasure but a very solemn ceremony. Early in the morning, the village sends to invite the headmen of neighboring villages to come. A long and beautiful poem is recited. They reply with another poem and then come to take part in the magic. They are seated on special mats at north, south, east, and west according to where the villages are situated. Then the rest of the men form a circle around them. The headman recites a long poem, telling how the magic liquor produces the white clouds, the rain and "the thick stalk, the broad leaves and the fair tassel" of the corn. Then the liquor in huge baskets is passed around the circle. To each of the headmen, another speech is made and he responds with a song about rain and clouds.

Plate 39. Passing cactus liquor in basket at rainmaking ceremony.

In this way, the dark red juice is solemnly drunk until the jars are empty. People say that in the old days there was no more drinking but now each family brews a jar of liquor at home and invites friends to come and try it. The custom is that whoever has a gourd full of liquor offered him must "cover it with a song," and all the Papago know some of these songs about the rising of the clouds over the mountains and the coming of the frogs or the spiders who bring the rain.

After the rain ceremony, in old days the fields were planted. In some villages there used to be nightly singing to make the plants grow. The people would make images of corn, beans, and squash out of carved wood or clay or stone, and all the older men would sit around them singing songs of growth.

During the summer, in former times, everyone was too busy for ceremonies. But after the crops were in and while there was still water in the water pools, came the great time for merry making. It was at this time that the village challenged another to races or kickball contests. The challenge took place in spring and the young men had probably been practicing all summer. Now in the autumn, the game leader went to the game leader of the rival village and announced the contest in ten days time. This contest was not a mere athletic meet. The challenging village generally sang a series of songs to the opponents and since the songs were thought to bring good luck, the opponents paid for them in food and goods. Probably the challengers had also been practicing songs during the summer and they might have sent for some man who was a famous song composer to teach his special set of songs and train the young boys and girls in a dance that would illustrate them.

When the time for the games arrived, almost the whole village marched to the place of contest. They camped outside it and sent a messenger to say they had arrived and next morning they marched in, in state, painted and singing. They went to the dance ground and gave their musical performance. Sometimes this amounted almost to an operetta. The old men, who were usually the singers, sat at one side of the dance ground with baskets turned upside down as drums. They topped these with sticks and sang while some twenty boys and girls did the dancing. The young people had their long, black hair flowing loose; they wore only the usual costume of skirt or breechclout but their bodies were painted perhaps in dots to represent corn or splashes for corn leaves or even with bluebirds or rainbows. In their hands they carried cleverly made objects to illustrate the song.

The Papagos had little material for toy making but they contrived birds out of raw cotton; rainbows out of bent painted sticks; clouds of fluffy cotton; even mountains of white buckskin on a frame of sticks.

The young people circled the dance place, two by two, in a skipping motion for this was called the skipping dance. Some of the spectators, if they like, might run out and dance beside them and the relatives of the young people paid them. When the dance was over, the women of the challenged village came out with cooked food as pay for the dancers. This was not only a reward for their entertainment but because the songs would bring rain and food to the village whose name had been mentioned.

Sometimes a special set of songs was sung called Naming songs. This meant that different members of the challenged village were mentioned by name and since such mention brought them luck, they were expected to pay. The challengers had a series of songs, some about headman, some for medicine men, some for warriors. They inquired the night before, the names of the prominent men in the challenged village and then practiced fitting them into the songs. One of their old men made a bundle of sticks, each stick standing in his mind for one of the names to be mentioned. During the singing, he sat with sticks in front of him and as he called out each name for the singers to use, he laid down a stick. Every man whose name was mentioned, provided a pile of food for the singers and it was quite the thing for his wife to present it by chasing the singers and throwing tortillas at them.

Then came the really important part of the entertainment, the games. Often the first was a relay race in which every able-bodied man in each village took part. The track was a cleared space on the desert and there were umpires and starters for each side. The men might run all the afternoon before the race was finally decided. At other times the contest was kickball over a course which might amount to twenty or thirty miles. Three or four men kicked on a side with horsemen riding beside them to encourage them. The women might play shinny or have a relay race of their own and usually the old people played dice and guessing games. Enormous amounts of property were bet, the challengers bringing with them every basket, piece of buckskin and horse that they could spare. Though the challenged people had paid a good deal in the way of food, they might, if they were lucky, get back a good deal more from betting on the games.

During the races, the goods which had been wagered were placed in a pile: all matched in pairs. If one man wished to bet a horse, he found a horse bet from the opposite side and the two were tied together. In the same way, two pieces of buckskin were tied and two baskets of beans piled one on the other. When the outcome was decided, the winner took the pair.

THE DEER DANCE:

Another ceremony which always took place in the autumn just before the people moved to the winter village was called the deer dance or the cleansing ceremony. Its object was to work magic over all the crops which had been gathered and over the first deer of the season, to make them safe for eating during the winter. Hunters went out to look for the deer and to shoot them but on this occasion the deer head disguise was not used. In one village, it was considered wrong to shoot the deer. The men simply surrounded him in a narrow circle and then a special man who held the position from his father, strangled the deer without shedding blood. The deer tail was considered a magic property and was taken back to the council house to be used in curing. This was one of the few occasions when the two halves, Buzzard and Coyote, had some importance for a Coyote man must carry the deer tail, and the Buzzard man the meat. The meat was cooked by the old women, one Buzzard and one Coyote, and in some villages it was hung on a pole in the dance grounds. The old men sang while the young men and women, painted to represent the corn, danced in a long line in front of the deer meat and the heaped up vegetables. Sometimes the young men carried arrows as a symbol of the deer, and the girls, corn ears. The songs were all about deer hunting and were supposed to make the deer easy to kill in the future.

When the dance was over, the young people washed off the paint in cold water and, in some places, they fasted for four days so that the magic of the dance would not harm them. The deer meat was distributed to all the people and each one as he took his piece, begged of it "Keep me well; let me have no sickness."

Sometimes a ceremony, a little like the deer dance, was given later in the winter to keep illness from the people. The deer which was their principle meat food was thought always to be a cure for sickness and so a deer was killed and the deer songs sung. Then the medicine man took a branch of some very thorny cactus and walked into the houses where there was sickness. The idea was that sickness would cling to the cactus, which he then carried out and buried. Besides that, he might drive a stick into the ground, reciting a long poem which told how sickness was being driven down and buried.

VIKITA, THE EAGLEDOWN FESTIVAL:

There was another very important feast which followed the deer dance. In the north of the Papago country it was held only every four years but in the south, every year. This was called Vikita and might be translated "Prayer Stick" festival. It was both a thanksgiving feast and a blessing of the crops to make sure that they would grow in the future and that everything would be well. In the north of the Papago country, five villages joined and each had a leader who must know the sacred recitations which had come to him from his father. Also each had a man who composed eight songs for the ceremony and who directed the making of a huge image of clouds or deer or something that stood for food. These images were to be carried in procession by a number of dancers.

Long before the ceremony, the song composers were notified and began to get their material together. Then only ten days before it the leader of the whole ceremony gathered the other village leaders and went to open the sacred basket kept at Archie, the oldest village, and the one where the ceremony always took place.

The basket contained small sticks with tufts of eagle feathers attached to them by string. These were to be presented to all people at the feast to place in their fields and make the crops grow. When it was opened, the feast leader made a solemn recitation about the coming of the rain and clouds; often he announced to all the people who had gathered to watch, that the feast would be held in ten days and that all must go home and work at the preparation. He and his four assistant leaders after this had to fast and pray in preparation for their sacred duties. The Papago had no sacred house where this could be done so each man went into the desert alone and made himself a small fire. In this solitary camp, he spent all his time when not directing the feast preparations; but in the daytime each leader was instructing the men of his village in singing and preparing the images to be used.

At each village, the men built a special round enclosure where they would work out of sight of the women. Here the song composers brought the materials for their images and they taught the young men of the village the eight new songs. Every image was to be carried by ten or twelve men who would wear masks made out of gourds. Their long hair would be flowing and their bodies painted to represent corn kernels. Their only garment was a small kilt of home-woven cotton which came to the knees.

All the young men wanted to be singers and offered themselves for practice. If they had no masks, they made them at this time but many had masks which had been in the family for generations. They worked all day in the enclosure, hardly speaking above a whisper and always stooping when they moved. No woman must enter but their wives and mothers might bring food and leave it outside the door.

For this feast there were always a number of men dressed as clowns in white buckskin masks and short white skirts. They wore their costume during the whole time of preparation and it was their duty to run about among the houses and beg for food for the working men. The clowns were supposed to be holy beings from a magic country who spoke a language none could understand. Therefore, they never really talked but gave strange, shrill cries. Certain men in every village had inherited, from their fathers, the right to be clowns and cherished it as a sacred privilege. The idea of the clown at a sacred ceremony is a very old one among Indians. He is not thought to be making fun of the ceremony but to represent a magic being so powerful that he may behave as he likes while mere men must be reverent. These clowns were thought to bring with them the seeds of the squash and to have power to make them grow; and they could also take away disease by merely touching people because they were connected with all life and growth.

There were other officers busy with the fast preparations, and these were the Sprinklers of Cornmeal. Corn, which was the staple food of the Papago as of many

Indians in the Southwest, was regarded as holy. To sprinkle a little cornmeal on anyone or anything was the same as giving him a blessing. So the Cornmeal Sprinklers, whose office ran in certain families, stood at the doors of the enclosure where the men were working and sprinkled anyone who went out on an errand so that his work would be blessed.

When the final day came, people from all the five villages crowded to Archie. In the old days they went on foot, now they go in wagons. At Archie, a huge round enclosure had been built so that the singers from each village might camp inside with their leaders. Women, whose duty it always was to carry wood and water, ran ahead of the singers and made a pile of wood for them in their own part of the enclosure. This was the only work that women might do in a festival which belonged to men. As the company from each village arrived, the clowns from the other villages surrounded them, listening to the songs they were singing and trying to remember the words; but the home clowns drove them off with a mock battle. Then the singers camped in the enclosure and the rest of the people outside.

The feast began before sunrise next morning. The first act, for it was almost a theatrical performance, was the appearance of two masked men who represented the sun and moon. The Sun carried a round shield of buckskin painted with a face; while the Moon had a square shield. They walked out just as the sun was rising and circled the enclosure, stopping to bend to and fro in imitation of the movements of the heavenly bodies. Behind them came the Cornmeal Sprinklers, blessing them with cornmeal. After this, there was a series of processions which lasted all day.

In the huge enclosure, with its door to the east, the singers of each village masked and painted themselves. Then came the first group from the first village, which was always Archie, singing their first song. Ahead of them walked a Sprinkler of Cornmeal, blessing the ground on which they would walk. Then came a little boy masked like the old singers and carrying a rod with a bluebird feather at the end. After him came the twelve young men, carrying a platform made of cactus ribs on which there might be a great image of a cloud or a mountain made of buckskin with small carved birds upon it; or perhaps a deer or a giant cornstalk. Every song composer had one subject which he always used from year to year so whatever the image was, he had composed a song to illustrate it. The young men sang this song as they danced with the image on its platform, and behind them came two more Cornmeal Sprinklers to cover their tracks with blessing.

They danced around the village square and stopped in front of the ceremonial house, which was a domed building of grass like all the other village dwellings. Here two young men and two girls stood dancing all day long, holding arrows and ears of corn to symbolize meat and vegetable food. The procession stopped before them to sing and threw cornmeal over them while the Cornmeal Sprinkler who stood beside them blessed the procession in his turn. In this way the singers from Archie came out with eight different images and sang eight songs. Then each of the other four villages, in turn, sent out its eight images of food and good fortune. The spectacle lasted until the day was over.

When the procession paused at noon, all of the clowns came out and sometimes the five villages provided thirty altogether. They gave a little drama, making fun of the village ceremonies and of all the daily acts. Everyone was expected to laugh at the clowns and yet the People themselves would never have dared to make fun of sacred things in this way. The clowns with their power to do this, frightened people as well as amused them. Everyone connected with the ceremony was thought to have holy power and many sick people came to be cured by merely touching the singers or the clowns or the small boys with their bluebird wands.

When the last songs were sung and the people were ready to separate, the prayer sticks from the sacred basket were given out. Every man who wanted one might put it in his field and the power of growth and life which came from the ceremony would make the field fertile. In this way, if he placed the stick in his house thatch, it would keep the family well and happy.

Another Prayer Stick festival was held at the south of the Papago country, which is now in Mexico. This feast still takes place every year in August but it is not so elaborate as the one at the north. Still all the villages from the southern part of the country come to the built-in enclosure at Quitovaca. They send out their singers, two at a time instead of twelve, and carry feathered wands instead of huge images; but they are masked like the men in the north and the Cornmeal Sprinklers go before and follow them. They sing of rain and clouds and all the blessed things which make human life happy and their songs are thought to bring good luck to their villages.

While they sing, old men of Quitovaca sit under their own arbor singing special songs. They have with them the sacred basket which belongs to their town and which is said to contain half the heart of a monster who once tried to devour them. The monster was killed by Itoi, their protector, and the heart given them for a memento. It is in charge of an old woman whose family has always kept this basket and who must sit all day without eating while they do it honor. When the feast is over, the basket is taken back to the hills.

The ceremonies we have been describing were for the purpose of bringing rain, or making the crops grow, or calling the deer. In fact they were to get food which was the first thought of people living in such a barren country. The songs they used are said to be those which Elder Brother gave the people when they first needed rain and food. The songs are very beautiful, brief but very vivid pictures of the running deer and the tasselled corn. Besides them, there are recitations something like prayers. These describe the needs of the first people and the way they were satisfied, with the rain and the corn for which they asked the gods.

Then from the east a wind arose,
Well knowing whether it should blow.

All kinds of clouds together
Their heads upreared
And with it, they did go.
Pulling white feathers from their breasts, they went.

These poems, with their moving descriptions of the rain, which was the very life of the people, are some of the most beautiful in any Indian language.

But the Papago had another need besides food. Every man wanted to feel, within himself, the power to work and fight and endure hardships. The belief of the People was that all nature is full power: the birds, the animals and even the plants can do strange things which men cannot do. If man wishes power, he will gain their favor.

VISIONS:

Papago grandfathers told their grandsons that if they were virtuous and hard-working, some day an animal would speak to them and tell them some of his magic. This magic was always a song, for the Papago believed that it was by singing that man brought the rain, and drove away sickness, in fact, accomplished all good things. So every boy, when he was out on the desert alone, watched for the hawk or the mountain lion which might suddenly stand beside him and speak with a human voice.

But there were other ways to get power. Certain things which a man could do, the Papago thought, were so dangerous and so mysterious that they brought a man directly in contact with the unknown. Three things seemed to them of this sort. The first was taking the scalp of an enemy. The Apache who were the regular enemies of the Papago had a habit of rushing upon them suddenly in the winter rain when it was hard to catch them. They took captives and hurried away to the mountains almost before a village knew it had been attacked. So the Papago thought that they were witches and that an enemy's scalp had terrible power.

Another thing which they found mysterious was the distant ocean, so different from the waterless land where they lived. They went once a year to the shores of the Gulf of California to gather dried salt, and they felt that the sight of the waves and the touching of them was another magic experience.

The third was the killing of an eagle. The eagle, to many Indians, is a sacred bird and some say that he is a god who finally took this form. To kill him is therefore a bold act. But if one dares do it, his feathers are magic, for the downy feathers are so like clouds that they bring the rain; the wing feathers are used by the medicine men to brush away disease; and the tail feathers are deadly for war arrows because the eagle is so brave.

So the Papago felt that if they had taken a scalp, or gathered salt from the seashore, or killed an eagle, they had come in touch with magic. A man who had done any of these things must stay away from other human beings because the terrible power which was pouring through him might hurt them as well as him. He must go alone into the desert and stay for sixteen days—four was the sacred number and four times four was particularly magic.

While the young man went into the desert, he must eat only a very little; he must not look at the sun or at fire; he must not touch his hair except with a special stick. The People, like many Indians, felt that the hair represents the man and that to touch it when one is in a magic state is dangerous. The young man who was in this condition had an old man who took care of him. This guardian came every day to tell him ancient stories and recite the poetry which described fasts of other men who had done the same as he. When the old man was gone, the young one sitting alone, waited for some dream in which he would learn a song, giving him power as a great runner or a hunter or fighter. Beside him, as he waited, hung his bow and arrow if he had taken a scalp; or shells from the sea if he had been a salt gatherer; or the eagle feathers if he had killed an eagle. These things were magically dangerous just as he was and they must be sung over before they would be safe for human beings to touch.

When the sixteen days were over, he was taken back among his fellow men. All the men who had been through the same experience as he, gathered together. Then

Plate 40. Enemy killer, fasting in desert, his weapons beside him.

his old teacher brought him to sit with them while they sang the magic songs that they themselves had learned while they were dreaming. They sang all night, one man after another. Then each went up to him in turn and blew tobacco smoke over him. Tobacco in these ancient times was not a pleasure: it was an incense which was given to the gods and which made them inclined to help human beings. The smoke was thought to purify the young man and take the danger from him. As the older man smoked, he called the young one by some term of relationship, for in small Papago villages every one was related. Then the old man made a wish, "My nephew, you will be like me; you will be a great hunter; you will run in the mountains; you will always find game; you will kill it; and so take care of your family." Or if the smoker had been a famous runner or a fighter or a healer, he wished these things for his young relative.

61

A man who had been through such an experience as this was called a "ripe man." Now he was ready to speak in council meetings and to be respected. It was a very different idea from that of many Indians and many Whites. Generally, the feeling is that when a man has done a brave act he should be given praise and gifts. Very few people take the attitude of the Papago, that the hero should be humble and should, in fact, be afraid of his power until he has tested himself and is sure he can use it well.

When those interested in the Pima inquire if they had the same sort of visions, we find it hard to tell. They certainly had the same arrangements as the Papago about a man who killed an enemy. Perhaps their rules were even more severe. Old accounts tell how the killer, among the Pima, did not sit still waiting for a vision but wandered about with his teacher, half starving, while all the people kept away from him. When White American soldiers came into the Pima country, they found the Indians very friendly and they often used their help as scouts against the Apache. The Pima were brave but every time one of them killed Apache, he had to leave the fight and spend sixteen days getting purified. The White soldiers were not used to this. Finally they had to give up using Pima scouts.

As for the salt gathering and the visions that came after it, this was a Papago custom. If you ask the Pima about it, they always say: "We know nothing. Salt belongs to the Papago." In fact the Papago, after their salt had been blessed, used to take some of it and trade with the Pima. The Pima paid for their salt with wheat and corn and cotton but they never got any visions from it.

The Pima, today, say nothing about getting visions from killing an eagle. Perhaps they once did and there may even be old people who know something about it. No one has found them, however, and we have to leave it that we know nothing about eagle visions with the River People.

THE MEDICINE MAN:

There were certain people in a Papago village who had special power to cure disease, to bring rain, to tell when the enemy was coming, even to tell when their side would win in games. These were the medicine men. A medicine man got his power by dreams just as other men did but he began very young and kept dreaming and hearing new songs until long after he was a grown man. Sometimes he took scalps; gathered salt or killed eagles like the others but generally he did not try to be a warrior. But he might go for salt and have strange visions of medicine men under the sea who took him to their houses and told him about disease, or he might kill eagles year after year, always getting new visions. He never told what he had dreamed for that would destroy his power. Even his family did not really know what was happening, although they might hear him singing alone at night and understand that he was not like other boys. When he was a grown man and had thought over his dreams a long time, he might tell people that he was ready to practice as a doctor.

Plate 41. Medicine man's bag containing crystals.

Most Papago medicine men did not do any curing. Their business was only to tell what had caused the disease and then someone else who knew the right songs could cure. The medicine man, in order to know what was the matter, had to sing all night beside his patient and sometimes for many nights. He sat down cross-legged with his gourd rattle in one hand and two long eagle feathers in the other. He shook the rattle and sang softly in a strange voice that no one could understand—songs about the visions that had come to him. Then he brushed the evil from the patient with the eagle feathers and blew over him the purifying tobacco smoke. Sometimes he carried in a little bag three or four crystals which he called his shining stones. He said that they gave him light to see like a torch so that he knew where the sickness was. Perhaps he laid them down and watched to see how they threw their light; then he sang, waving his plumes and smoking, until morning.

Plate 42. Image of horned toad, carried by singer who cured horn toad disease.

At last, he might say "It is the owl sickness;" "It is the badger sickness;" "It is the deer sickness." Then the family paid him, for medicine men were always paid more and sooner than anyone else. He went away and now it was the business of the family to find someone who knew owl songs or badger songs or deer songs. Any man in the village might sometimes have had a dream where one of these animals sang to him and everyone would know about it. So the singer would be sent for and if several had songs from the same animal, they would all come. They might perhaps bring an image of the animal, which had helped them, to make their singing more powerful.

63

The Papago idea was that animals, who understood the world so much better than man, have the power to send disease. They do so if man has treated them cruelly or wastefully; if he has killed them with too much suffering or if he has not shown respect to their caves and holes. The animals know that they are man's food and are willing to be killed. But, if man is wasteful or cruel, the animals are angry and punish him. However, they always find some men whom they like and they come to these men in visions, showing them how disease can be cured. So every village has several men—or it did in the old days—who know songs to cure some disease. One will know the songs for the badger disease, another for the deer disease. Perhaps there are two or three men who have songs for the same disease, but all different songs. As soon as the family of the sick person knows what disease he has, they send for one of these curing singers to come and sit by him. Often the curing singer has a claw or a feather or a little image of the animal whose song he knows and he brushes this over the patient in blessing. If the disease has not too firm a hold, this singing is expected to work a cure. The curing singer is not paid like the medicine man. He works out of neighborly kindness and all he gets is his food while he is singing.

Just a few medicine men can cure as well as locate the disease. These men sometimes blow the disease away and sometimes they suck at the patient's body because they feel something dangerous has got inside him. This is an idea like the modern idea of microbes, except that the method of treatment is different.

In the old days, medicine men were said to have power not only to locate disease but also to bring rain and work other magic. A medicine man always sat within the circle while the people were singing for rain, waving his eagle feathers to find from which direction the rain was coming. Hunters used to take a medicine man to the mountains because they said he could see the deer before it came and warriors took him to tell them where they would meet the enemy. Before the big games between villages, the medicine men used to sing songs to make the other side lame and blind. Sometimes they held great contests to show which village had the most power. Rival medicine men would swallow sticks like swords and eat coals and the one who could do the most was sure that his village would win.

But because the medicine man could do so much, the people were afraid of him. They felt that he might work witchcraft for killing people as well as curing them. Sometimes if a man had had a great many patients die, the villagers would be sure he was working evil magic and then with the consent of the council, they would go out with their clubs and kill him.

PAPAGO AND PIMA TODAY

THE PAPAGO and Pima have known the White men for almost two hundred and fifty years. It was in 1687 that the first Spanish missionary Father Eusebio Kino, established headquarters in the Altar Valley in Mexico. Then he began making journeys north to get acquainted with the unknown Indians living there. On these journeys, he brought the seeds of such Spanish vegetables as wheat, chick peas, onions, watermelons, and melons. He presented them to the Indians and he showed them the way they were cultivated by the Spaniards of that time. It is owing to Kino's teaching that the Papago still thresh wheat with horses as the seventeenth century Spaniards did.

Kino also introduced the Indians to horses, cattle, and sheep, the first they had seen. They were quick to see the usefulness of these animals and many of them have had horses and cattle ever since, though the country was rather too hot for sheep. The Papago, in particular, took to the raising of cattle until it is now their main industry.

Most of the Indians, at this time, were converted to the Catholic faith. Kino established a few missions in the country where the Papago now live and they continued for a while after his death. But they could not attend to nearly all the people and headquarters were still in Mexico. Many of the desert Papago used to go for the winter to these Mexican missions, where they would have their children baptized with Spanish names and have instruction in Christian doctrines. When they went home, they carried on church services as well as they could for themselves. They called themselves the sonora (or Mexican) Catholics and they are still using their own churches and their own services. Also they make a trip to Mexico once a year, choosing the little town of Magdalena, south of Nogales; here they stay for a week or two just as they did in old Spanish days. They bring with them the picture of their special saint, Saint Francis of Assissi, to be blessed.

There were never any missions in the Pima country and those among the Papago at last died out. A new missionary who was a Franciscan, not a Jesuit like Kino, came for a while to Bac, which is now San Xavier, outside Tucson, He found the Indians still devoted to the church and it was even after his time, about 1800 that the beautiful church which now stands at San Xavier was built by them.

But in 1821 Mexico became a republic and there were no more missionaries sent to the Indians. Soon after that, the United States and Mexico had a little war and the peace treaty gave a piece of Arizona to the United States. It was the country

Plate 43. Modern Papago house.

north of the Gila River where the Pima live and the United States thought it was not enough. In 1854 they bought another strip. That took in what is now the southern part of Arizona, down to the Mexican border. It left the Pima in the United States with part of the Papago while the other part was south of the Mexican border, where they still are.

Now came the time of the gold rush to California and White men started stream-ing along the trails of Arizona. Most of them came through the Pima country because there they could get water while the Papago country was a place where no one dared to live but a Papago. So the Pima began to speak English, take American names, and wear American clothes while the Papago more often spoke Spanish.

The Pima, too, had water so they began to raise wheat and even cotton while the Papago kept on with their Indian corn, beans, and squash. But the Papago desert was good grazing country for cattle so the herds began to grow until now the Pima are mostly farmers while the Papago are cattle raisers.

In 1870 a reservation was set aside for the Pima on the Gila River where they still are. But the Papago still were little known. They were given a small reservation at San Xavier, where the Santa Cruz River gave them water in 1874. In 1883, they got another at Gila Bend, up near the Pima. It was only in 1917 that the government set aside the large reservation in the desert, where most of the Papago live. This is called the Sells Reservation.

This Sells reservation was the last of all large Indian reservations to be established. It was on the very land where the Papago had always lived and there were no treaties or payments connected with it. It was simply marked off so that Papago could continue to have their own country, without fear that White ranchers would fill it up. Since the reservation was set aside, more land has been added to it from time to time. Deep wells have been dug in many villages, so that the people no longer have to move when summer is over. Many reservoirs have been dug and tanks have been set up. The Papago country is no longer so hard to live in as it used to be.

There are over five thousand Papagos now, in the three reservations. Their business is mostly farming and raising cattle. However, some of them go out to work in the copper mines or the cities of the White people. Lately, they have had government work on roads and dams. There are government schools and mission schools on the reservations and most young Papago speak English. But they all speak their own language too. There are many who still tell the old stories, carry on old ceremonies, and sing the old songs. They even make new songs, as beautiful as the old.

Plate 44. Painted seed jar and rough cooking jars.

SHORT LIST OF READING ON THE PIMA AND PAPAGO INDIANS

Castetter, Edward and Ruth M. Underhill
The Ethnobiology of the Papago Indians. University of New Mexico, Ethnobiological Studies in the American Southwest, no. 2.

Culin, Stewart
Games of the North American Indians. Bureau of American Ethnology, Report No. 23.

Curtis, Edward S.
The North American Indian, vol. 2. The Plimpton Press, Norwood, Mass.

Densmore, Frances
Papago Music. Bureau of American Ethnology, Bulletin No. 90.

Hoover, J. W.
Generic Descent of the Papago Villages. American Anthropologist, vol. 37, no. 2, 1935.

Kissell, Mary Lois
Basketry of the Papago and Pima. Papers of the American Museum of Natural History, vol. 17, part 4, 1916.

Lumholtz, Carl
New Trails In Mexico. New York, 1902.

Russell, Frank
The Pima Indians. Bureau of American Ethnology, Report 26.

Underhill, Ruth M.
Singing for Power, the Song Magic of the Papago Indians of Southern Arizona. University of California Press, 1938.

Underhill, Ruth M. (continued)
Autobiography of a Papago Woman. Memoirs of American Anthropological Association, no. 48, 1936.

A Papago Calendar Record. Bulletin, University of New Mexico, 1938.

Social Organization of the Papago Indians. Columbia University Contributions to Anthropology, 1939.

Those interested in further study should consult the bibliographies of the publications listed above.

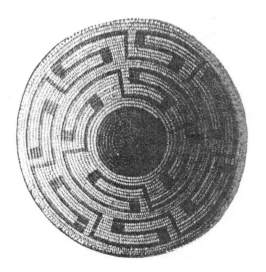

LIST OF ILLUSTRATIONS

INDIAN LIFE AND CUSTOM BOOKS

In 1935 Superintendent Donald Biery of Sherman Institute invited Dr. Ruth Underhill to offer a summer program in anthropology on his campus for Indian Bureau teachers. The plan was a success, and in the year that followed, Sherman Institute received many requests for material about the Southwest Indian tribes which had been the subject of Dr. Underhill's courses. She was asked to prepare materials to answer these questions, which Sherman mimeographed and distributed. Later, Haskell Institute published the materials in printed form.

In preparing and revising her material, Dr. Underhill has had the generous cooperation of members of the Bureau of American Ethnology, of the Southwest Museum, Los Angeles, the Art Museum, Los Angeles and the Laboratory of Anthropology, Santa Fe. The Bureau of American Ethnology has made available its photograph file, and Velino Herrera, a Pueblo artist, has traveled with Dr. Underhill through Pima and Papago country in the preparation of his many drawings.

These books have been prepared to furnish an understanding of Indian life and customs before the coming of the White man, and to show some of the impact of White culture on native habits and beliefs. Written primarily to satisfy the questioning of Indian children who desire to know about their tribal history, they should inform employees of the Indian Bureau about the culture patterns underlying Indian behavior, as a basis for better understanding between the races. They may also serve to answer many of the questions White children throughout the United States are asking about Indians.

Willard W. Beatty

Plate 45. Bow made of boxthorn or mulberry